W9-AUI-504

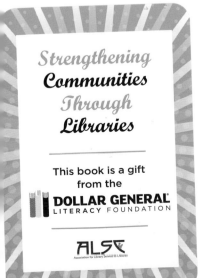

Strengthening
Communities
Through
Libraries

This book is a gift
from the

**DOLLAR GENERAL**
LITERACY FOUNDATION

ALSC
Association for Library Service to Children

dabblelab

PAPER AIRPLANES
with a SIDE of SCIENCE

# NEEDLE NOSE!

## ADVANCED-LEVEL
### Paper Airplanes

by Marie Buckingham

4D An Augmented Reading
Paper-Folding Experience

CAPSTONE PRESS
a capstone imprint

# TABLE OF

# CONTENTS

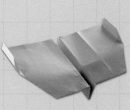

## Download the Capstone 4D app!

**Step 1**  Ask an adult to search in the Apple App Store or Google Play for "Capstone 4D."

**Step 2**  Click Install (Android) or Get, then Install (Apple).

**Step 3**  Open the app.

**Step 4**  Scan any of the following spreads with this icon. - - ➔ ★

When you scan a spread, you'll find fun extra stuff to go with this book! You can also find these things on the web at *www.capstone4D.com* using the password: planes.nose

# PREPARE FOR TAKEOFF

Welcome aboard! You've earned the rank of pilot, and you're ready to fly. Just a reminder: Check the lightbulb boxes tucked alongside the paper airplane instructions for bite-size explanations of flight-science concepts related to your models. Check the photo boxes for tips on how to best launch your finished planes. And remember, there are four main forces that airplanes need to fly successfully: lift, weight, thrust, and drag. But the eight paper airplanes in this book need one more thing: YOU!

# MATERIALS

Every paper airplane builder needs a well-stocked toolbox. The models in this book use the materials listed below. Take a minute before you begin folding to gather what you need:

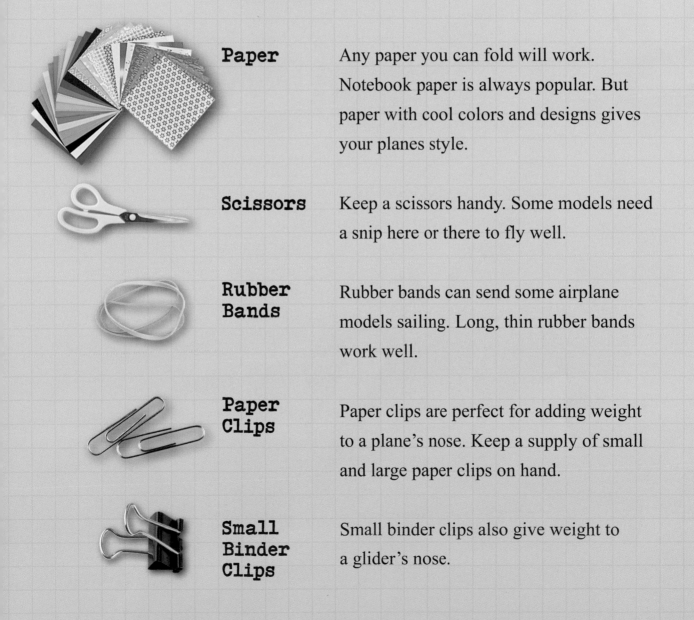

**Paper** — Any paper you can fold will work. Notebook paper is always popular. But paper with cool colors and designs gives your planes style.

**Scissors** — Keep a scissors handy. Some models need a snip here or there to fly well.

**Rubber Bands** — Rubber bands can send some airplane models sailing. Long, thin rubber bands work well.

**Paper Clips** — Paper clips are perfect for adding weight to a plane's nose. Keep a supply of small and large paper clips on hand.

**Small Binder Clips** — Small binder clips also give weight to a glider's nose.

# TECHNIQUES AND TERMS

Folding paper airplanes isn't difficult when you understand common folding techniques and terms. Review this list before folding the models in this book. Remember to refer back to this list if you get stuck on a tricky step.

**Valley Folds**

**Valley folds** are represented by a dashed line. The paper is creased along the line. The top surface of the paper is folded against itself like a book.

**Mountain Folds**

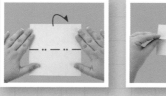 

**Mountain folds** are represented by a pink or white dashed and dotted line. The paper is creased along the line and folded behind.

**Reverse Folds**

**Reverse folds** are made by opening a pocket slightly and folding the model inside itself along existing creases.

## Mark Folds

**Mark folds** are light folds used to make reference creases for a later step. Ideally, a mark fold will not be seen in the finished model.

## Rabbit Ear Folds

**Rabbit ear folds** are formed by bringing two edges of a point together using existing creases. The new point is folded to one side.

## Squash Folds

**Squash folds** are formed by lifting one edge of a pocket and reforming it so the spine gets flattened. The existing creases become new edges.

# FOLDING SYMBOLS

Fold the paper in the direction of the arrow.

Fold the paper behind.

Fold the paper and then unfold it.

Turn the paper over or rotate it to a new position.

A fold or edge hidden under another layer of paper; also used to mark where to cut with a scissors

# ⭐ LIFTOFF

## Designed by Christopher L. Harbo

Ever wish you could put more power behind your launch? Your wish is granted with this plane. The notch in Liftoff's nose is strong enough to withstand the pull of a rubber band. Get ready. Aim. Fire away!

## Materials

* 8.5- by 11-inch (22- by 28-centimeter) paper
* scissors
* rubber band

## FLYING TIP

Hook the plane's notch onto one side of the rubber band. Hold the other side of the rubber band with one hand. Pull back on the tail of the plane with the other hand. Stretch the rubber band as far as it will go and release.

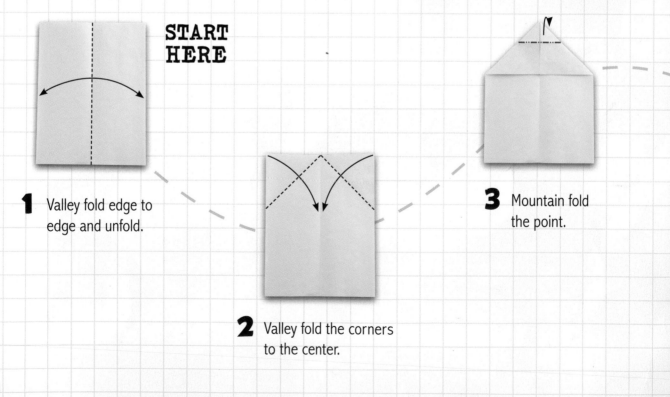

**START HERE**

**1** Valley fold edge to edge and unfold.

**2** Valley fold the corners to the center.

**3** Mountain fold the point.

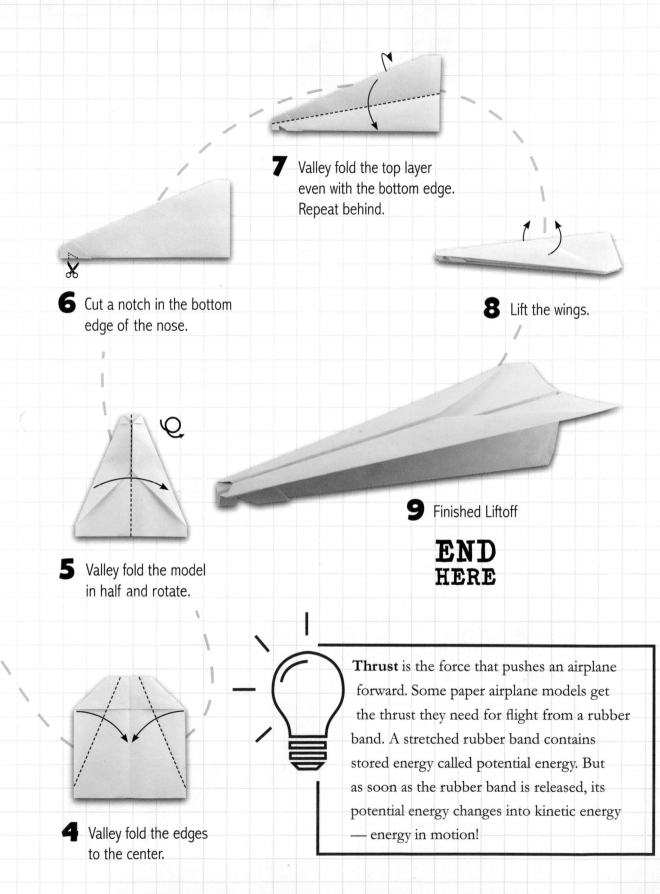

**7** Valley fold the top layer even with the bottom edge. Repeat behind.

**6** Cut a notch in the bottom edge of the nose.

**8** Lift the wings.

**5** Valley fold the model in half and rotate.

**9** Finished Liftoff

# END HERE

**4** Valley fold the edges to the center.

**Thrust** is the force that pushes an airplane forward. Some paper airplane models get the thrust they need for flight from a rubber band. A stretched rubber band contains stored energy called potential energy. But as soon as the rubber band is released, its potential energy changes into kinetic energy — energy in motion!

# ★ NEEDLE NOSE

## Traditional Model

It's not hard to figure out how the Needle Nose got its name. This model's pointy beak gets damaged easily. But the plane's awesome flights will make up for the time you spend straightening the nose.

## Materials

* 8.5- by 11-inch (22- by 28-cm) paper

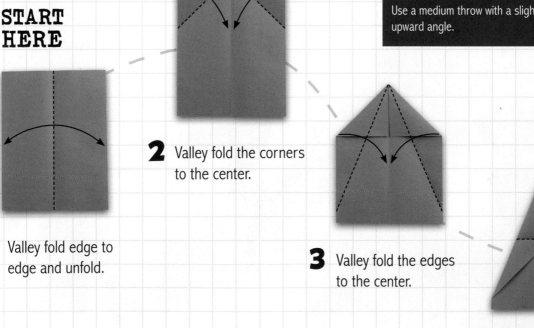

**START HERE**

**1** Valley fold edge to edge and unfold.

**2** Valley fold the corners to the center.

**3** Valley fold the edges to the center.

**4** Valley fold the point.

As an airplane soars through the sky, a force called **drag** pushes against its forward movement. Drag is caused by air rubbing against a plane's surface. Airplanes with thin, sleek noses experience less drag upfront, which means a faster flight!

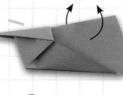

**8** Lift the wings.

**9** Finished Needle Nose

# END
## HERE

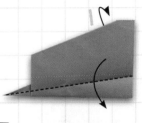

**7** Valley fold the top layer. Repeat behind.

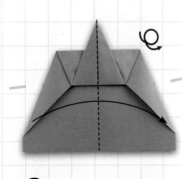

**5** Valley fold the point. Note how the crease is even with point A.

**6** Valley fold the model in half and rotate.

# ⭐ AVIATOR

## Traditional Model

The Aviator is one cool mini jet. This model looks like a dart and has a built-in cockpit. With a strong throw, you might think a tiny pilot is guiding it across the room.

## Materials

* 6-inch (15-cm) square of paper

Most fighter jets have joysticks in the cockpit. A joystick is used to operate an airplane's **ailerons** and **elevator**. Ailerons are small, hinged fins on the end of wings that help a plane turn by rolling. An elevator is a moveable surface on a plane's tail. It causes up and down movement of the nose, called pitch.

**START HERE**

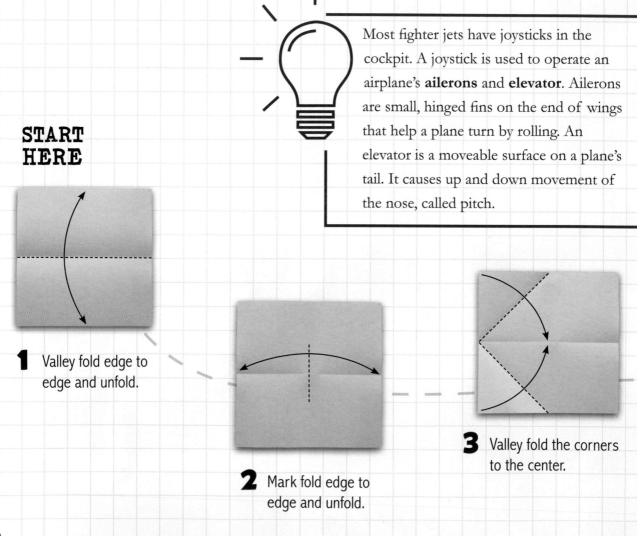

**1** Valley fold edge to edge and unfold.

**2** Mark fold edge to edge and unfold.

**3** Valley fold the corners to the center.

**5** Valley fold the edges to the center.

**6** Mountain fold the model in half.

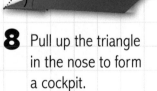
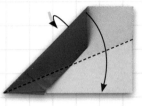

**7** Valley fold the top layer even with the bottom edge. Repeat behind.

**4** Mountain fold the point to the mark made in step 2.

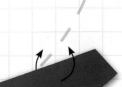

**8** Pull up the triangle in the nose to form a cockpit.

**END HERE**

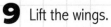

**9** Lift the wings.

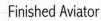

**10** Finished Aviator

13

# ★ FANG

## Designed by Christopher L. Harbo

Tiny teeth give the Fang a dangerous look, but this gentle glider won't bite. The plane's light wings are at the mercy of air currents. In flight, it sways from side to side as it crosses a room.

## Materials

* 8.5- by 11-inch (22- by 28-cm) paper

The **weight** of an airplane is the downward force that pulls it toward the ground. **Lift** is the upward force created by air moving around a plane's wings. Lift must be greater than weight for an airplane to take off and fly.

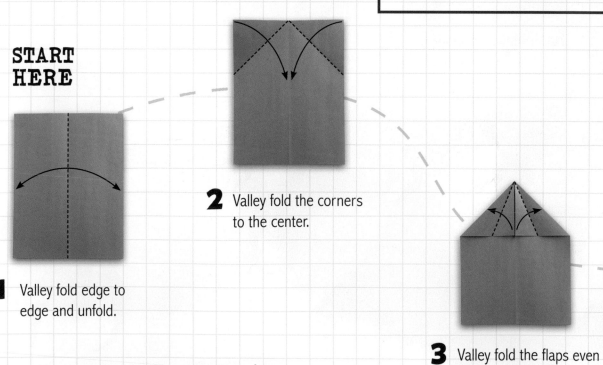

**START HERE**

**1** Valley fold edge to edge and unfold.

**2** Valley fold the corners to the center.

**3** Valley fold the flaps even with the outer edges.

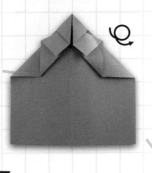

**7** Turn the model over.

**6** Valley fold the top corners to the center. Allow the tiny flaps behind the corners to release to the top.

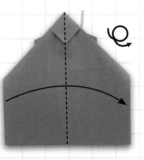

**8** Valley fold the model in half and rotate.

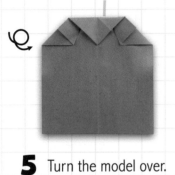

**5** Turn the model over.

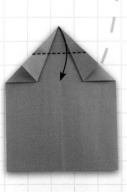

**4** Valley fold the point.

**9** Valley fold the top layer. Repeat behind.

**Continue** ▶

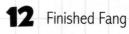

**12** Finished Fang

## END HERE

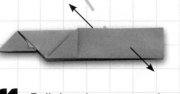

**11** Pull the wings outward to unfold.

**10** Valley fold the wing even with the top edge. Repeat behind.

## FLYING TIP

Use a medium, level throw.

# LAZY LANDER

## Designed by Christopher L. Harbo

Make way for the Lazy Lander! This plane gets its magic from the binder clip. Placed under the nose, the clip gives the glider the weight it needs to fly. Better yet, the clip's legs can serve as landing gear.

## Materials

* 8.5- by 11-inch (22- by 28-cm) paper
* small binder clip

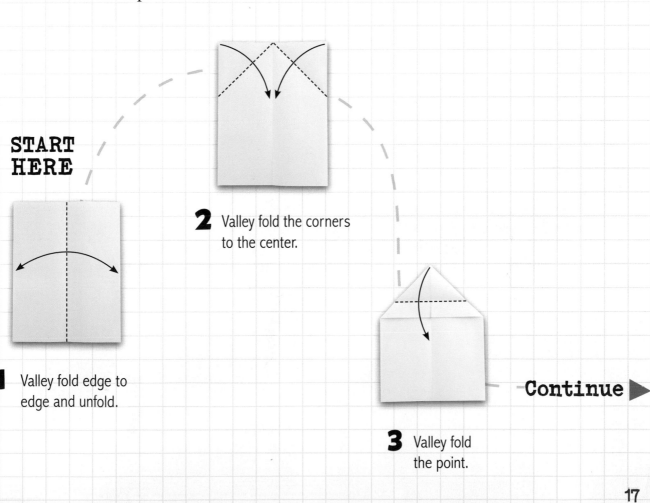

**START HERE**

**1** Valley fold edge to edge and unfold.

**2** Valley fold the corners to the center.

**3** Valley fold the point.

Continue ▶

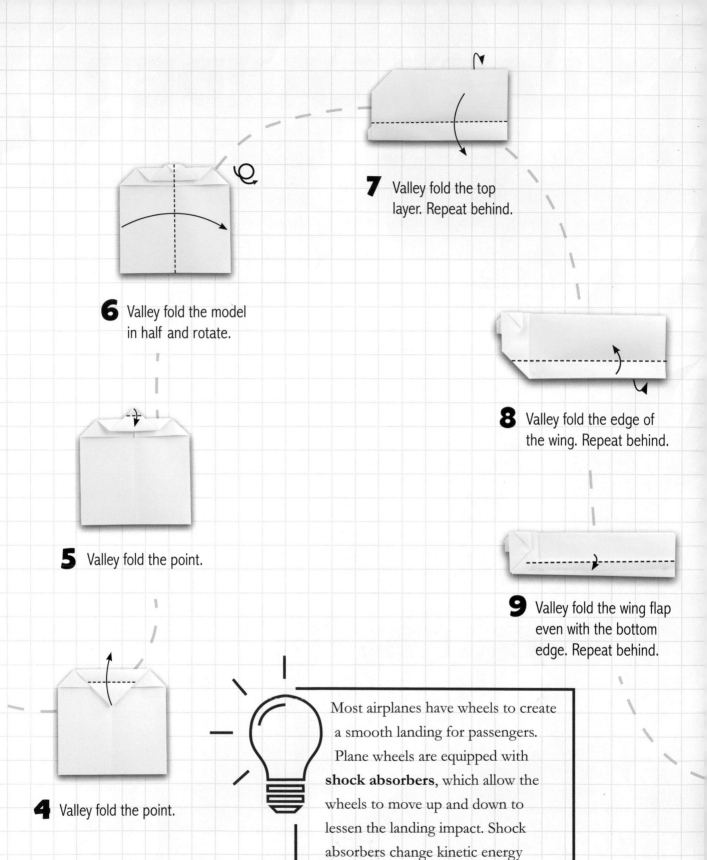

**7** Valley fold the top layer. Repeat behind.

**6** Valley fold the model in half and rotate.

**8** Valley fold the edge of the wing. Repeat behind.

**5** Valley fold the point.

**9** Valley fold the wing flap even with the bottom edge. Repeat behind.

**4** Valley fold the point.

Most airplanes have wheels to create a smooth landing for passengers. Plane wheels are equipped with **shock absorbers**, which allow the wheels to move up and down to lessen the landing impact. Shock absorbers change kinetic energy (energy in motion) into another type of energy — heat.

**END HERE**

**13** Finished Lazy Lander

## FLYING TIP

Use a medium, level throw.

**12** Add a binder clip to the front of the plane.

**10** Lift the wings.

**11** Pull the wing flaps up and out to the side.

# ★ HANG GLIDER

## Traditional Model

The Hang Glider takes you soaring to new heights.
With the right throw, this glider climbs into the air.
When it can go no higher, it banks to the side and
curves around the room.

## Materials

* 10-inch (25-cm) square of paper

**START HERE**

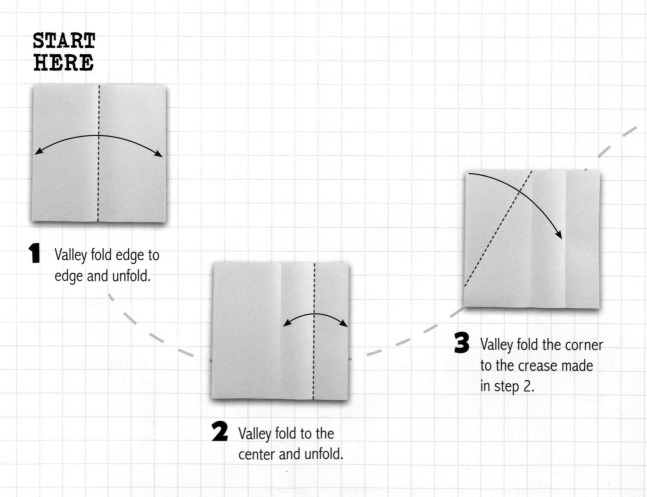

**1** Valley fold edge to edge and unfold.

**2** Valley fold to the center and unfold.

**3** Valley fold the corner to the crease made in step 2.

20

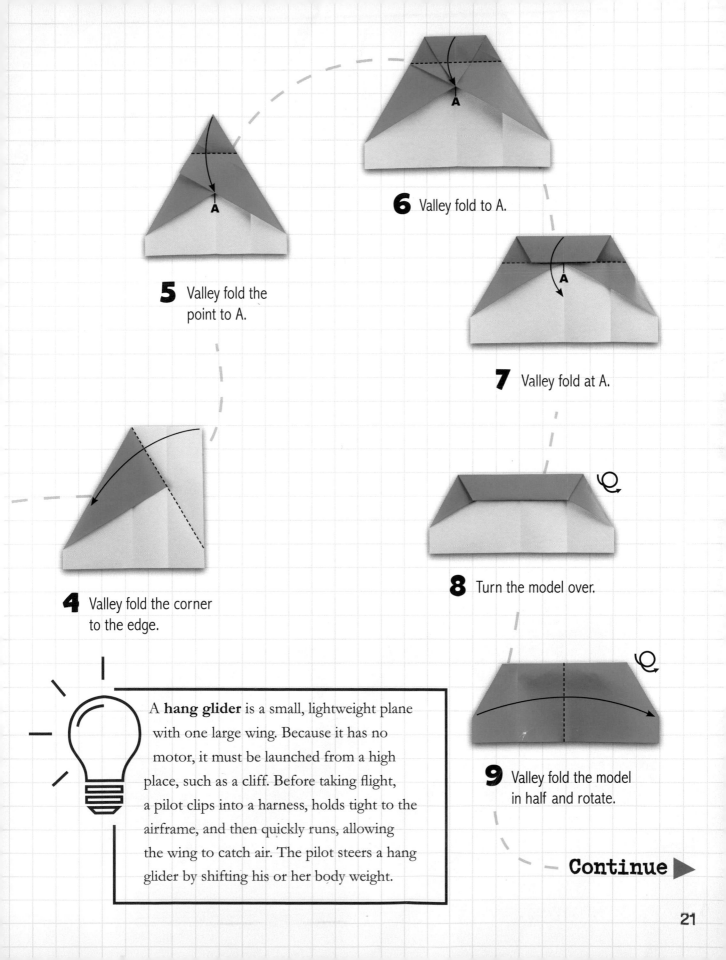

**6** Valley fold to A.

**5** Valley fold the point to A.

**7** Valley fold at A.

**4** Valley fold the corner to the edge.

**8** Turn the model over.

A **hang glider** is a small, lightweight plane with one large wing. Because it has no motor, it must be launched from a high place, such as a cliff. Before taking flight, a pilot clips into a harness, holds tight to the airframe, and then quickly runs, allowing the wing to catch air. The pilot steers a hang glider by shifting his or her body weight.

**9** Valley fold the model in half and rotate.

Continue ▶

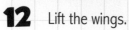

**12** Lift the wings.

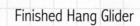

**13** Lift the wing flaps so they stand up at 90-degree angles.

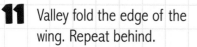

**11** Valley fold the edge of the wing. Repeat behind.

**END HERE**

**14** Finished Hang Glider

**10** Valley fold the top layer. Repeat behind.

## FLYING TIP

Use a medium throw with a slight upward angle.

# ⭐ STEADY EDDIE

## Designed by Christopher L. Harbo

Get ready for the Steady Eddie. Broad wings and slim wing flaps give this glider a smooth, stable flight. Two small paper clips beside the nose help guide the craft as it comes in for a landing.

## Materials

* 8.5- by 11-inch (22- by 28-cm) paper
* two small paper clips

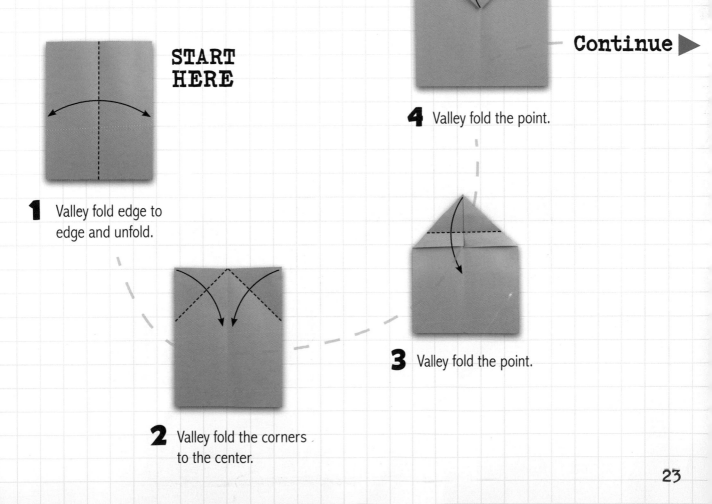

**START HERE**

**1** Valley fold edge to edge and unfold.

**2** Valley fold the corners to the center.

**3** Valley fold the point.

**4** Valley fold the point.

**Continue ▶**

23

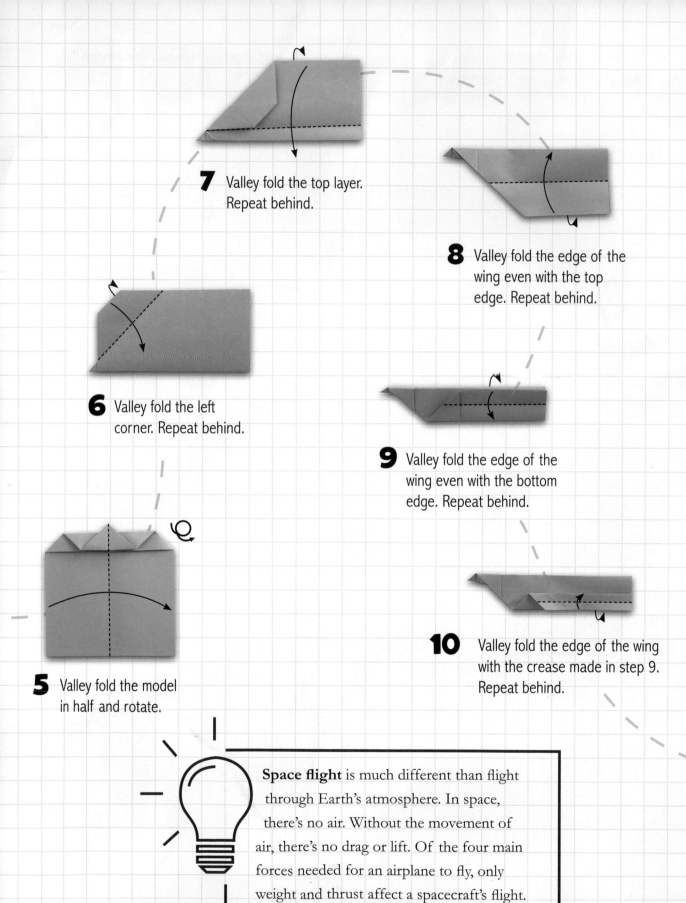

**7** Valley fold the top layer. Repeat behind.

**8** Valley fold the edge of the wing even with the top edge. Repeat behind.

**6** Valley fold the left corner. Repeat behind.

**9** Valley fold the edge of the wing even with the bottom edge. Repeat behind.

**5** Valley fold the model in half and rotate.

**10** Valley fold the edge of the wing with the crease made in step 9. Repeat behind.

**Space flight** is much different than flight through Earth's atmosphere. In space, there's no air. Without the movement of air, there's no drag or lift. Of the four main forces needed for an airplane to fly, only weight and thrust affect a spacecraft's flight.

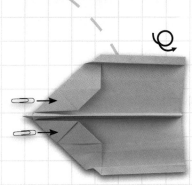

**13** Turn the model over.

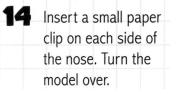

**14** Insert a small paper clip on each side of the nose. Turn the model over.

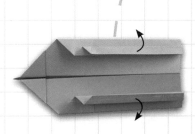

**12** Unfold the wing flaps on the creases made in step 8. Allow the edges of the wings to become L-shaped runners under the wings.

**11** Lift the wings.

**15** Finished Steady Eddie

## END HERE

25

# ★ D-WING

## Traditional Model

The D-wing's flight depends on how you release it. One flight might be long, smooth, and straight. The next might wobble, curve, and dive. It's a model that will keep you guessing.

## Materials

* 8.5- by 11-inch (22- by 28-cm) paper

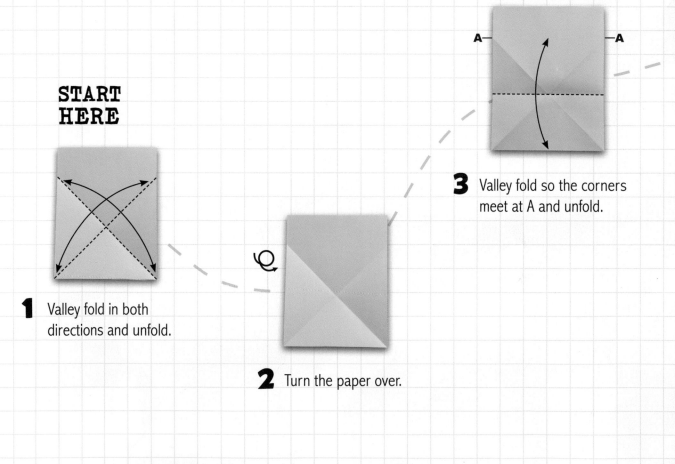

**START HERE**

**1** Valley fold in both directions and unfold.

**2** Turn the paper over.

**3** Valley fold so the corners meet at A and unfold.

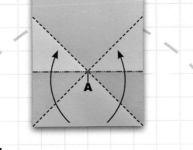

**5** Push at point A. Collapse the paper on the existing creases to form a triangle.

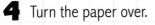

**4** Turn the paper over.

**6** Valley fold the top layers to the point and unfold.

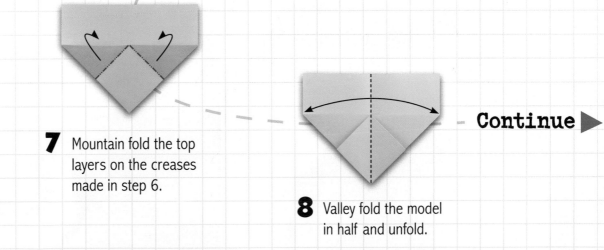

**7** Mountain fold the top layers on the creases made in step 6.

**8** Valley fold the model in half and unfold.

**Continue** ▶

Earth's gravity is the force that is constantly pulling objects with mass (including people) to the ground. Whenever someone slams on the brakes, blasts off in a rocket, or takes a sharp turn in a jet, he or she changes speed faster than gravity can pull. The measure of the change in speed is called **g-force**. High g-forces can be deadly. A person standing at sea level feels 1 G. Many race car drivers feel 5 Gs. Fighter jet pilots wearing special g-suits can endure 8 or 9 Gs.

**9** Valley fold the corners of the top flap to the center.

**10** Valley fold the point and unfold.

**11** Tuck the flaps into the pockets of the point.

## FLYING TIP

Pinch the back of the wing with two fingers and your thumb. The model will bend upward in the middle. Release with a strong forward flick of the wrist.

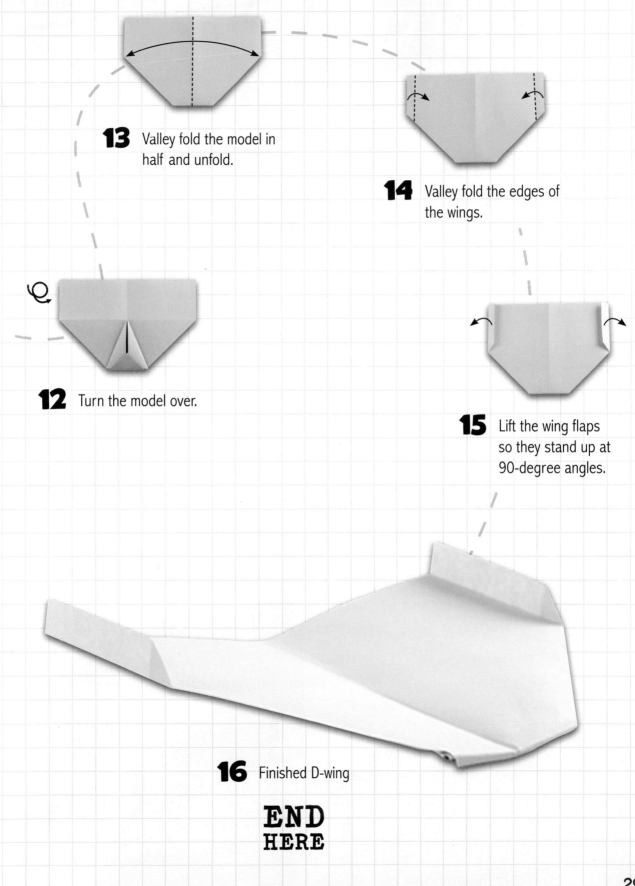

**13** Valley fold the model in half and unfold.

**14** Valley fold the edges of the wings.

**12** Turn the model over.

**15** Lift the wing flaps so they stand up at 90-degree angles.

**16** Finished D-wing

# END HERE

# ⭐ INSIDE THE HANGAR:
## Hang Gliders and Paragliders

Although a hang glider doesn't have an engine to produce thrust, this small flying craft can soar for hours. Made of a lightweight metal frame and canvas, it has a high lift-to-drag ratio. This means that the amount of lift created by the glider's wing is far greater than the drag created by the glider and its pilot.

Areas with consistently hot, dry weather are the best places for hang gliders to take long flights. When the sun's rays heat up the ground, the air above it expands and rises. The rising columns of air are called thermals. Thermals push up on a hang glider's wing and keep the craft in flight.

The Guinness World Record for the longest hang glider flight is 474.7 miles (764 kilometers). The pilot, Dustin Martin, made his incredible 11-hour flight from Zapata, Texas, to Lubbock, Texas, on July 3, 2012.

A hang glider is essentially one big wing.

A paraglider is similar to a hang glider. Both use thermals to fly, move at about the same speed, and are relatively easy to control. The biggest difference is that a hang glider has a rigid frame, whereas a paraglider is simply a harness hanging from a fabric wing.

# READ MORE

**Collins, John M.** *The New World Champion Paper Airplane Book: Featuring the Guinness World Record-Breaking Design, with Tear-Out Planes to Fold and Fly.* New York: Ten Speed Press, 2013.

**LaFosse, Michael G.** *Michael LaFosse's Origami Airplanes.* North Clarendon, Vt.: Tuttle Publishing, 2016.

**Lee, Kyong Hwa.** *Amazing Paper Airplanes: The Craft and Science of Flight.* Albuquerque, N.Mex.: University of New Mexico Press, 2016.

# INTERNET SITES

Use FactHound to find Internet sites related to this book.

Visit *www.facthound.com*

Just type in 9781543507959 and go.

Special thanks to our adviser, Polly Kadolph, Associate Professor,
University of Dubuque (Iowa) Aviation Department, for her expertise.

Dabble Lab Books are published by Capstone Press,
1710 Roe Crest Drive, North Mankato, Minnesota 56003
www.mycapstone.com

Library of Congress Cataloging-in-Publication data is available on the Library of Congress website.
ISBN: 978-1-5435-0795-9 (library binding)
ISBN: 978-1-5435-0799-7 (eBook PDF)

Summary: For young flight-school students who are ready to take the controls, "Needle Nose!"
delivers challenging paper-folding projects with step-by-step instructions and special 4D-component
support. Clear, informative sidebars and an "Inside the Hangar" feature explain the basic science and
engineering concepts related to flight.

Editorial Credits
Jill Kalz, editor; Heidi Thompson, designer; Eric Gohl, media researcher; Laura Manthe, production specialist

Photo Credits
Capstone Studio: Karon Dubke, all steps
Shutterstock: design elements, Alexandra Lande, 30

Printed in the United States of America.
010761S18